AN EVO 50™ PARENTING TOOL

LABRITA ANDREWS, ED.M.

The ABCs *of* Team-Based Parenting™

Family Journal for Kids

Foreword by Alana Andrews

This Journal Belongs To:

Our Family Team

Family Name ______________________

Parent / Caregiver ______________________

Parent / Caregiver ______________________

Child ______________________

Child ______________________

Child ______________________

Child ______________________

Self-Published by the Author
EVO 50, LLC
P.O. Box 650161
Sterling, Virginia 20165

Cover Design & Layout: LaBrita Andrews, Ed.M.

First Edition published 2025
Second Edition: 2026

For permissions, inquiries, and bulk orders:
Email: support@evo50now.com
Website: www.labritaandrews.com

ISBN: 979-8-9954879-1-3 (Paperback)
ISBN: 979-8-9954879-2-0 (eBook)

Printed in the United States of America

All research findings referenced in this book adhere to APA 7th Edition citation standards. Every effort has been made to accurately attribute concepts to their original sources to maintain academic integrity and ethical scholarship.

DISCLAIMER

This journal is for educational and informational purposes only and is not a substitute for professional advice.

EVO 50, LLC
P.O. Box 650161
Sterling, Virginia 20165

DEDICATION

For every family building something new—together.
For the parents choosing connection over control.
For the children learning that their voice has value.
And for the future we shape when we show up as a team.

This is Team-Based Parenting™ in motion.
This is what growth looks like—side by side, step by step, conversation by conversation.

Let this journal be your reminder:
The power is in the we.

FOREWORD

By Alana Andrews
Founder, So Positive, LLC
Author | Speaker
Student, The Wharton School, University of Pennsylvania

I grew up in a home where conversations weren't just casual exchanges—they were building blocks of confidence. Every single night, without fail, our family gathered at the dinner table—my parents, my siblings, and I—creating a sacred space where every voice mattered, every idea was heard, and every dream found its wings. My parents didn't just tell us to be confident; they showed us what it looked like through these intentional discussions and unwavering belief in each of us. They didn't just tell us to believe in ourselves; they created space for dialogue that made each of us know, deep in our souls, that we could do anything we set our minds to.

My mother, LaBrita Andrews, Ed.M., was at the heart of this. She didn't parent through control—she parented through connection. She understood that raising children wasn't about forcing a path; it was about creating an environment where each of us could recognize our own power through meaningful conversation. My father stood beside her, reinforcing that belief, ensuring that our home—especially our nightly family dinners—was a place where confidence was cultivated, not commanded.

In our home, we were never told who we had to be—we were simply reminded of who we were and what we could accomplish. And possibility became the language of our family. As the youngest, I watched my siblings graduate from college and pursue their dreams, each achievement reinforcing what our parents had always told us: anything was possible.

At age 7, when I shared my concerns about bullying at our dinner table, my parents didn't just listen—they helped me channel those feelings into a song and took me to a producer to record it. At age 9, our kitchen table conversations about making a difference led me to launch the Girls So Positive talk show because they taught me that my voice mattered.

In 10th, our family discussions about helping others inspired me to create SWEY, a sports drink for people with diabetes—because they raised me to believe that if I saw a problem, I had the power to solve it. At fourteen, I published Creating Confidence to share what they instilled in me. And when I set my sights on Wharton, our conversations at the table reinforced that I could get there because I was raised to believe in my own potential.

Team-Based Parenting™ isn't just about raising children—it's about raising individuals who know their worth. It's about parents who listen, who engage in meaningful dialogue, and who teach their children that their voice, their dreams, and their ideas matter. I never had to find confidence—I was raised with it through daily family dinners and conversations that shaped me and my siblings' future.

That is what this journal represents. It's not just a place for writing—it's a space for growing. It's about creating a home where children don't just follow rules but develop the self-trust to speak, reflect, and discover who they are through open, honest dialogue.

This is more than just parenting.
This is the foundation for generational confidence.
To every parent sitting with your child—and to every child holding this journal in your hands—your voice matters. Let it rise here.

Alana Andrews

A Note To Parents

This journal is designed to help you and your child connect through everyday conversations.

It is not about doing everything perfectly.

It is about showing up, listening, and creating space for your child's voice.

Use these pages to talk, reflect, and grow together.

LaBrita

About
The ABCs of Team-Based Parenting™
Family Journal for Kids

This companion journal was created with one bold belief in mind:

Children don't just need to be raised—they need to be heard.
The ABCs of Team-Based Parenting™: Family Journal for Kids is more than a journal.

It's a bridge between you and your child. An emotionally safe place for them to explore who they are, what they feel, and how they make sense of the world—with you by their side.

Inside, you'll find:

- Reflective prompts to spark meaningful conversations
- Confidence-building activities to encourage self-expression
- Emotionally intelligent exercises that support regulation and resilience
- Creative spaces that invite joy, imagination, and connection

This journal is designed to meet your child right where they are—whether they're just learning how to name their feelings or stepping into their independence.
Whether used at the dinner table, during quiet moments before bed, or as part of your family's daily rhythm, this tool helps you co-create an environment where your child's voice is seen, safe, and valued.

Because in Team-Based Parenting™, every child deserves to feel heard—and every parent deserves tools to help make that happen.

Let this be your shared space to grow together—one letter, one prompt, one empowered voice at a time.

How to Use These Journal Pages

Choose a time to sit together—after dinner, before bed, or whenever your family is most relaxed.

Let your child lead.

Listen more than you speak.

Use each page as a starting point for conversation, not a task to complete.

Return to pages as often as you like.

Why This Matters

Children don't just need attention.

They need intention.

The conversations you have here can shape how your child learns to express themselves, build confidence, and feel heard.

DESIGN YOUR FAMILY TEAM T-SHIRT

AND DISPLAY IT WITH EXCITEMENT!

DRAW 3 THINGS YOU'RE GRATEFUL FOR TODAY

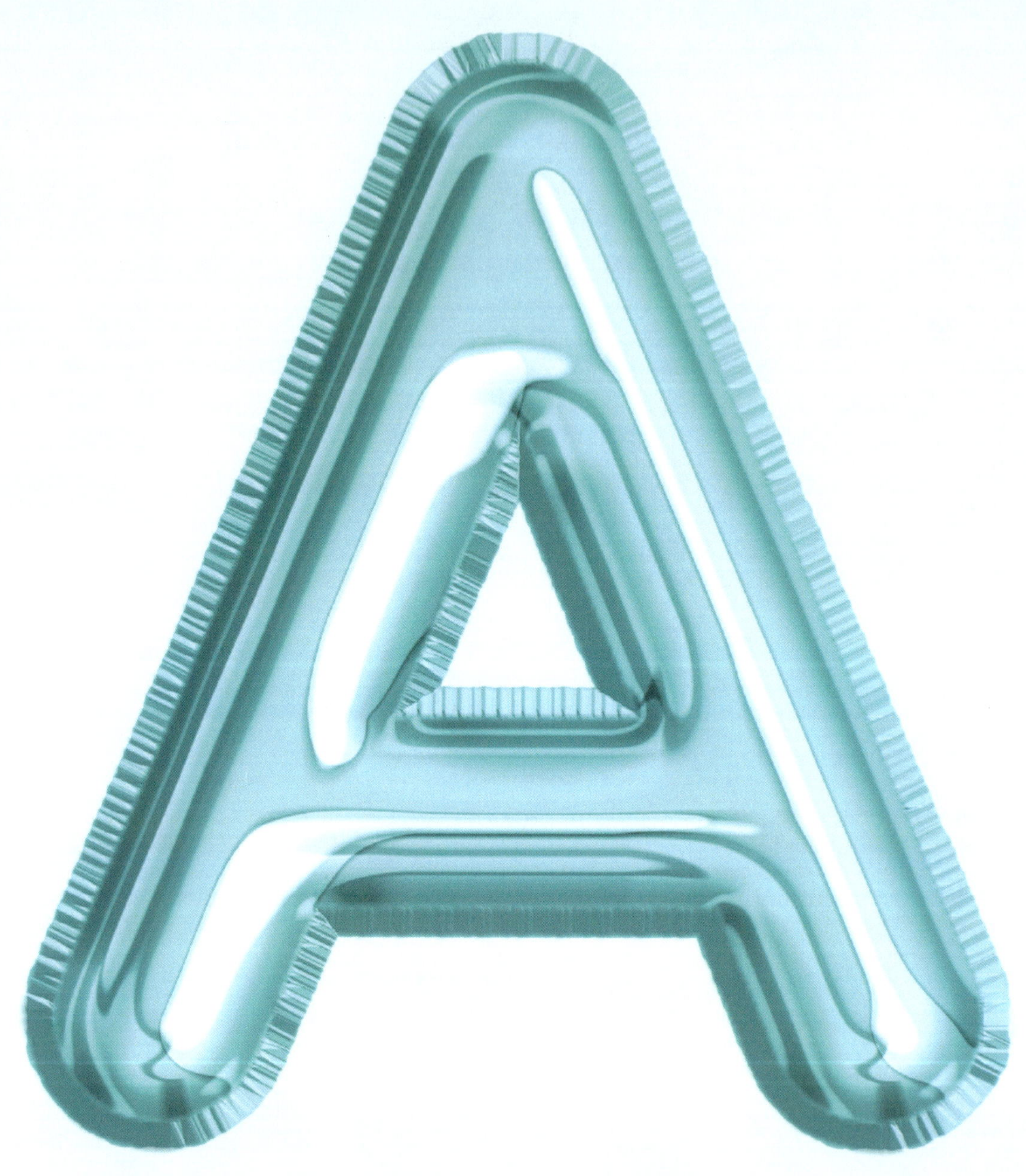

Art Projects Together

Collaborate on a family art project.

Choose a theme and let each family member contribute their own creative touch.

ACTIVITY

Engagement Idea

- Display everyone's work at home.

- Discuss each piece, celebrating individual creativity and the beauty of working together.

Words of Wisdom for Children

"CREATIVITY IS CONTAGIOUS, PASS IT ON."
-ALBERT EINSTEIN

Booktastic Family Fun

Choose books that interest all age groups.

Host family reading sessions where each member reads a part of a book aloud.

ACTIVITY

Engagement Idea

- Discuss the story's themes and characters.

- Encourage children to express their thoughts and feelings about the book.

Words of Wisdom for Children

"A BOOK IS A DREAM THAT YOU HOLD IN YOUR HAND."

- NEIL GAIMAN

Community Involvement

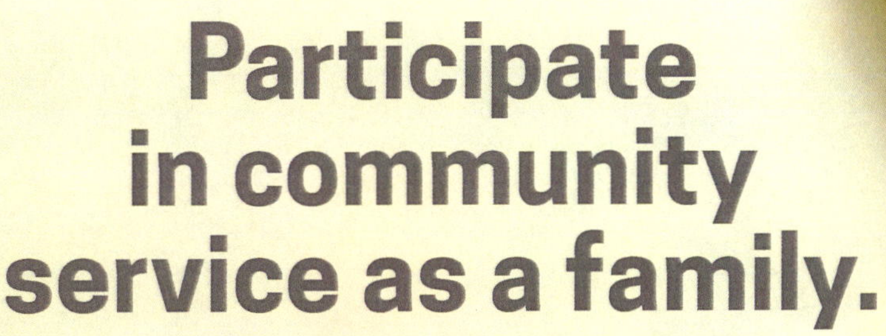

Participate in community service as a family.

This could include volunteering at local shelters, participating in clean-up drives, or helping at community centers.

ACTIVITY

Engagement Idea

- Let each family member choose a community activity.
- Reflect on these experiences and their impact.

Words of Wisdom for Children

"ALONE
WE CAN DO
SO LITTLE;
TOGETHER
WE CAN DO
SO MUCH."
-HELEN KELLER

Dance Party

Have a family dance party.

Let each member pick their favorite songs and dance together in the family's favorite space.

ACTIVITY

Engagement Idea

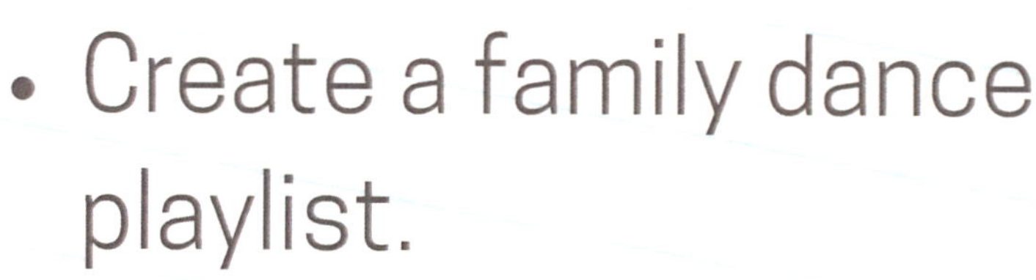

- Create a family dance playlist.

- Encourage each member to teach others their favorite dance moves..

Words of Wisdom for Children

"DANCE
IS THE HIDDEN
LANGUAGE
OF THE SOUL."
- MARTHA GRAHAM

Share Your Ideas

1.

2.

3.

4.

5.

Exploring Nature

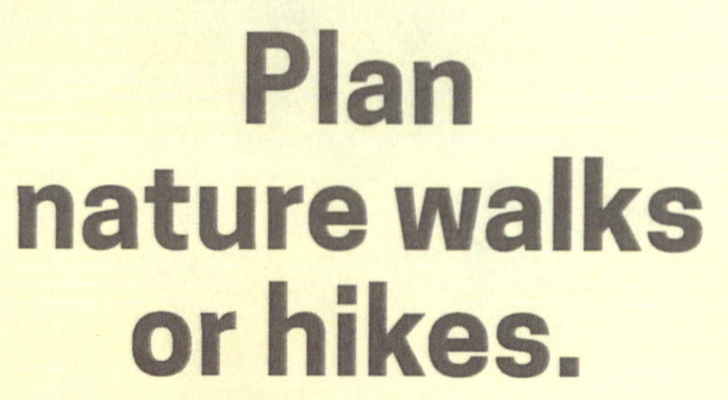

Plan nature walks or hikes.

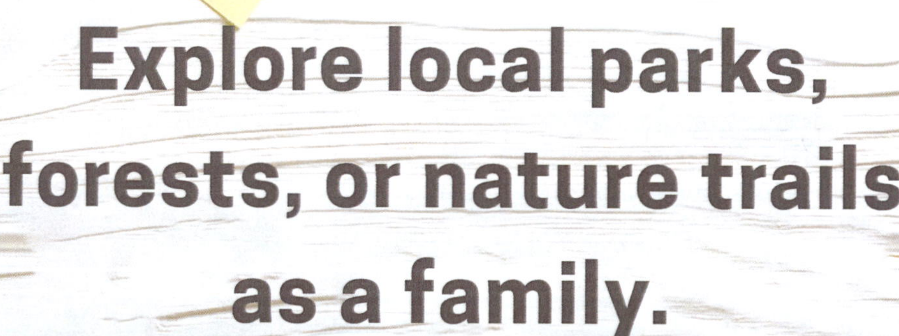

Explore local parks, forests, or nature trails as a family.

ACTIVITY

Engagement Idea

- Turn the walk into a scavenger hunt or a nature photography challenge.
- Discuss the importance of nature and environment.

Words of Wisdom for Children

"IN EVERY WALK WITH NATURE, ONE RECEIVES FAR MORE THAN HE SEEKS."

- JOHN MUIR

Family Fitness Challenge

Initiate a family fitness challenge.

Include activities like yoga, jogging, or cycling that can be done together.

ACTIVITY

Engagement Idea

- Set collective fitness goals.
- Celebrate when these goals are achieved to encourage a healthy lifestyle.

Words of Wisdom for Children

"THE BODY ACHIEVES WHAT THE MIND BELIEVES."

-UNKNOWN

Gardening Together

Start a family garden.

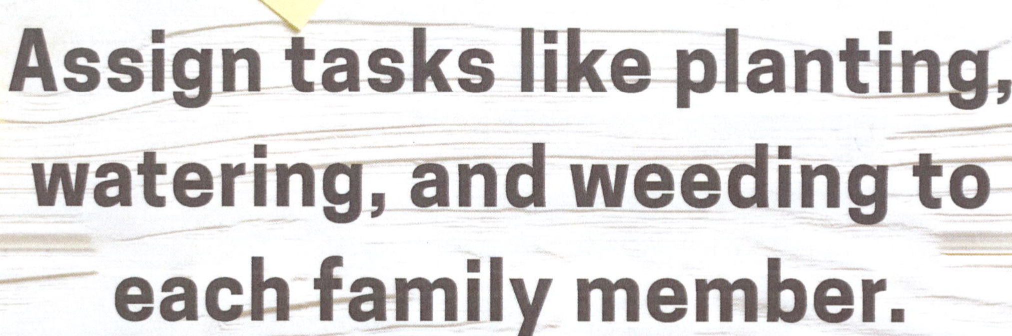

Assign tasks like planting, watering, and weeding to each family member.

ACTIVITY

Engagement Idea

- Choose plants or vegetables to grow together.
- Discuss the growth process and the care needed for each plant.

Words of Wisdom for Children

"TO PLANT A GARDEN IS TO BELIEVE IN TOMORROW."

-AUDREYHEPBURN

History Exploration

Learn about family history or explore local history together.

Visit museums, historical sites, or research family ancestry.

ACTIVITY

Engagement Idea

- Create a family tree.
- Share stories about ancestors or historical events in your local area

Words of Wisdom for Children

"HISTORY IS NOT JUST A SUBJECT; IT'S A JOURNEY THROUGH TIME."

- UNKNOWN

Share Your Ideas

1.

2.

3.

4.

5.

International Cuisine Night

Dedicate nights to cooking and enjoying international cuisines.

Let each family member pick a country and a dish to prepare.

ACTIVITY

Engagement Idea

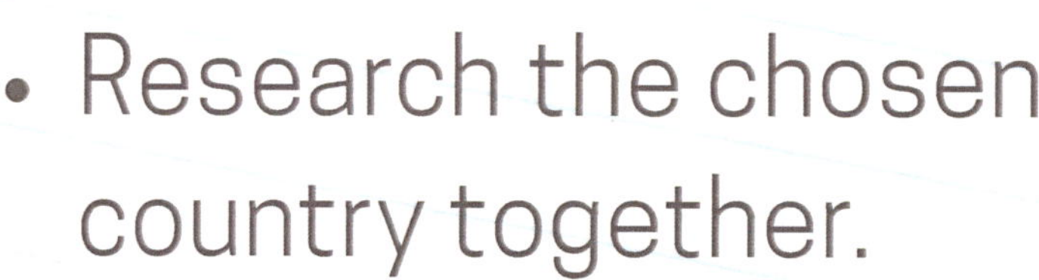

- Research the chosen country together.

- Discuss its culture and traditions while enjoying the meal.

Words of Wisdom for Children

"FOOD IS
THE INGREDIENT
THAT BINDS US
TOGETHER."
- UNKNOWN

Journaling Together

Start a family journal.

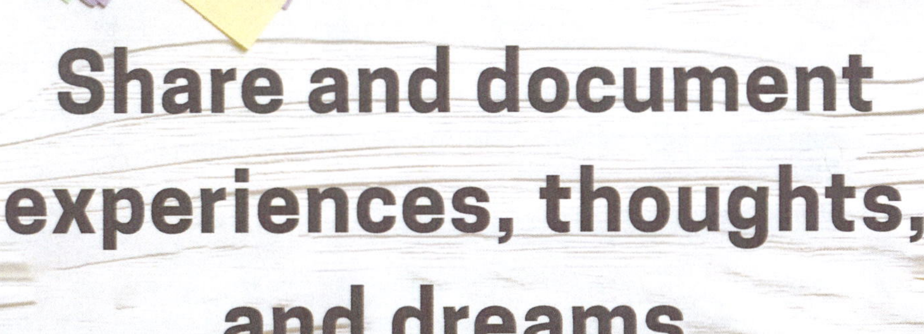

Share and document experiences, thoughts, and dreams.

ACTIVITY

Engagement Idea

- Regularly reflect on entries together.

- Encourage openness and understanding.

Words of Wisdom for Children

"JOURNAL WRITING IS A VOYAGE TO THE INTERIOR."

-CHRISTINA BALDWIN

Kitchen Science Experiments

Conduct simple, fun science experiments in the kitchen.

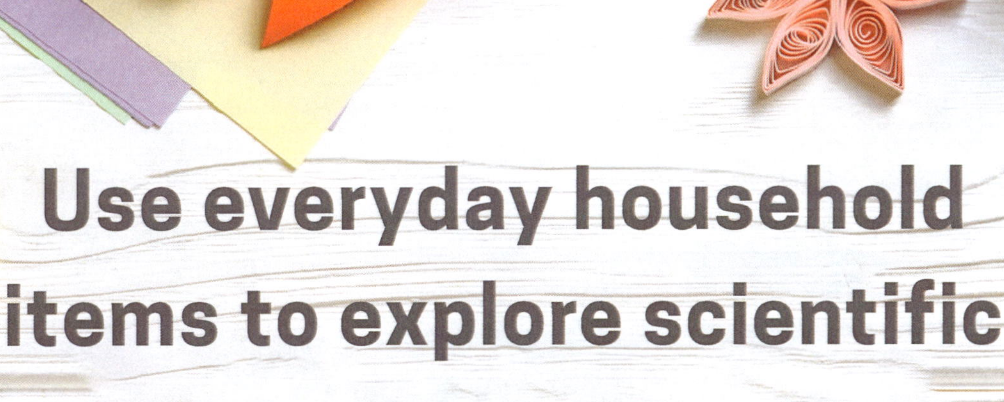

Use everyday household items to explore scientific concepts.

ACTIVITY

Engagement Idea

- Let children lead the experiments.
- Discuss the science behind each experiment and its real-world applications.

Words of Wisdom for Children

"THE SCIENCE OF TODAY IS THE TECHNOLOGY OF TOMORROW."

- EDWARD TELLER

Language Learning

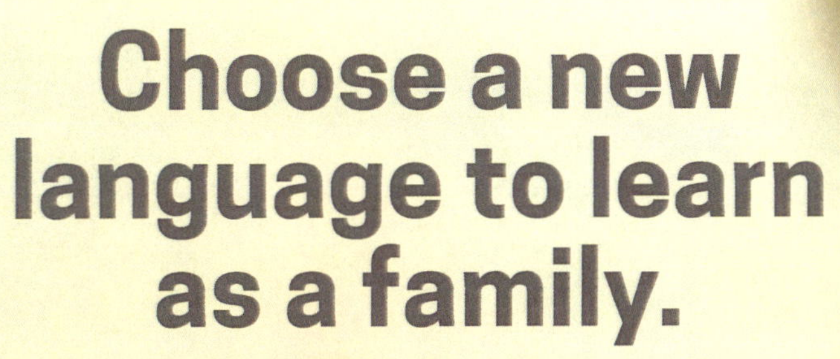

Choose a new language to learn as a family.

Use apps, books, or language classes to learn together.

ACTIVITY

Engagement Idea

- Practice the language during designated family times.

- Celebrate small milestones in learning with themed dinners or movie nights.

Words of Wisdom for Children

"ONE LANGUAGE
SETS YOU IN A CORRIDOR
FOR LIFE.
TWO LANGUAGES OPEN
EVERY DOOR
ALONG THE WAY."
- FRANK SMITH

Share Your Ideas

1.

2.

3.

4.

5.

Music Making

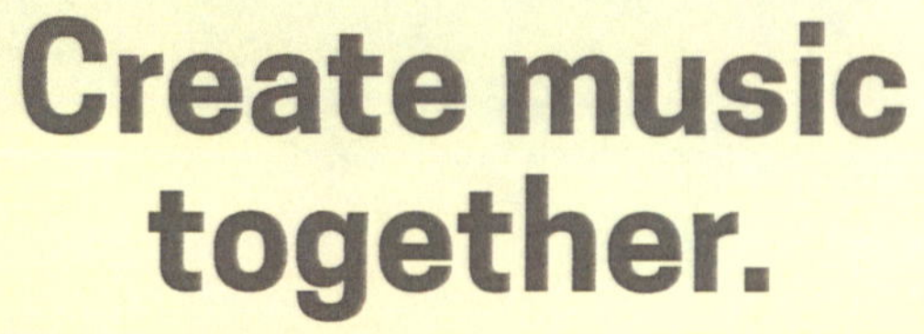

Create music together.

This can be as simple as singing, playing instruments, or even creating homemade instruments.

ACTIVITY

Engagement Idea

- Record your musical creations.

- Host a family concert to showcase your work.

Words of Wisdom for Children

"MUSIC
IS THE UNIVERSAL
LANGUAGE
OF MANKIND."
- HENRY WADSWORTH
LONGFELLOW

Nature Conservation Projects

Engage in conservation activities

like planting trees, building a birdhouse, or participating in recycling projects.

ACTIVITY

Engagement Idea

- Discuss the importance of each activity for the environment.
- Make it a regular family initiative.

Words of Wisdom for Children

"WE DO NOT INHERIT THE EARTH FROM OUR ANCESTORS; WE BORROW IT FROM OUR CHILDREN."

- NATIVE AMERICAN PROVERB

Outdoor Adventure Planning

Involve children in the planning process.

Plan outdoor adventures like camping, canoeing, or a day at the beach.

ACTIVITY

Engagement Idea

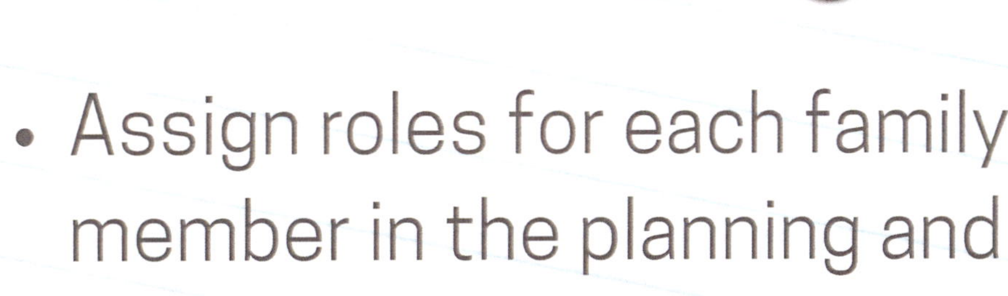

- Assign roles for each family member in the planning and execution.

- Reflect on these adventures in your family journal.

Words of Wisdom for Children

"ADVENTURE IS WORTHWHILE."
- AESOP

Puzzle and Game Nights

Organize regular family game or puzzle nights.

Choose games that require teamwork and strategy.

ACTIVITY

Engagement Idea

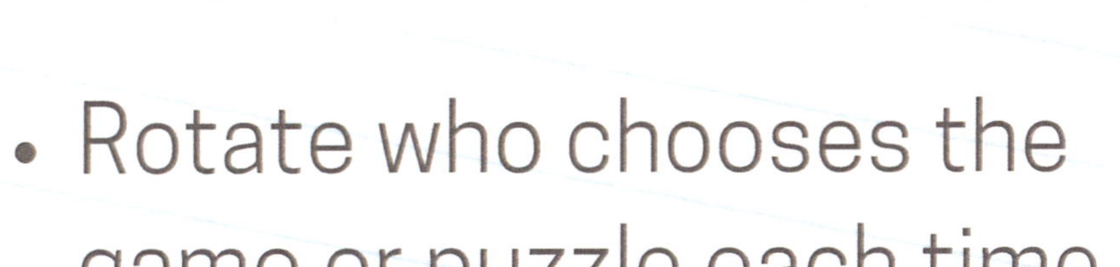

- Rotate who chooses the game or puzzle each time.
- Discuss the strategies used and lessons learned from each game night.

Words of Wisdom for Children

"EVERY PUZZLE PIECE PLAYS A PART IN THE BIG PICTURE."

- UNKNOWN

Share Your Ideas

1.

2.

3.

4.

5.

Quiet Time Reflections

Set aside regular quiet times

for individual reflection, followed by sharing insights with the family.

ACTIVITY

Engagement Idea

- Encourage each family member to share thoughts, feelings, or learnings from their quiet time.

Words of Wisdom for Children

"REFLECTION IS ONE OF THE MOST UNDERUSEDYET POWERFUL TOOLS FOR SUCCESS."
-RICHARD CARLSON

Road Trip Adventures

Plan family road trips to new destinations.

Involve everyone in choosing locations and planning the itinerary.

ACTIVITY

Engagement Idea

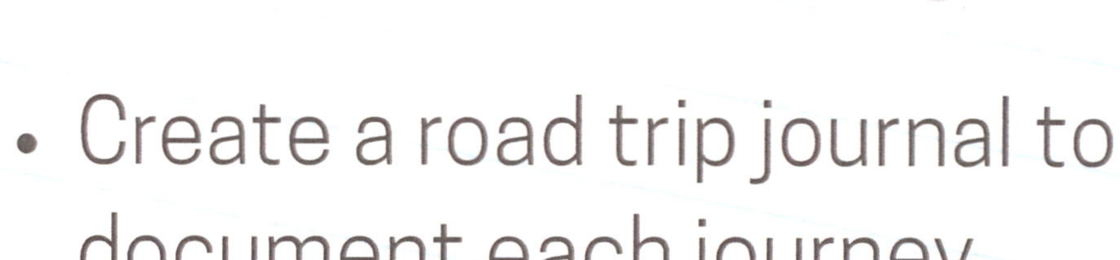

- Create a road trip journal to document each journey.

- Allow each family member to contribute with photos, drawings, or writings.

Words of Wisdom for Children

"THE WORLD
IS A BOOK,
AND THOSE
WHO DO NOT TRAVEL
READ ONLY
ONE PAGE."
- SAINT AUGUSTINE

Storytelling Sessions

Hold family storytelling sessions.

Share stories from your own life, create new stories together, or retell classic tales.

ACTIVITY

Engagement Idea

- Alternate who leads the storytelling.
- Discuss the morals, themes, and characters of each story.

Words of Wisdom for Children

"STORYTELLING IS THE MOST POWERFUL WAY TO PUT IDEAS INTO THE WORLD."

- ROBERT MCKEE

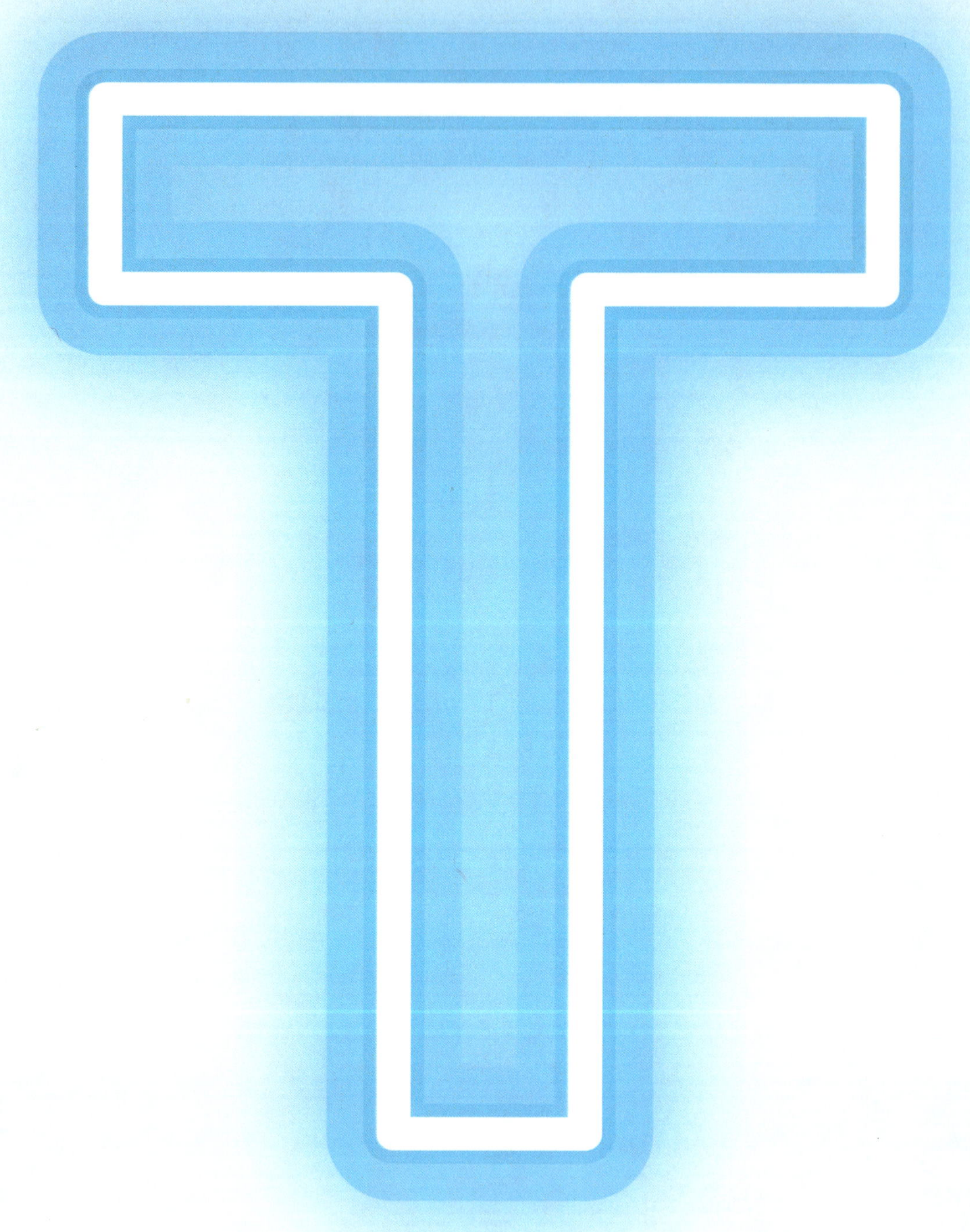

Talent Shows

Host family talent shows.

Encourage each member to showcase their talents, be it singing, dancing, magic tricks, or any other skill.

ACTIVITY

Engagement Idea

- Prepare for the talent show together.
- Celebrate each performance with positive feedback and encouragement.

Words of Wisdom for Children

"TALENT IS A GIFT
THAT BRINGS
WITH IT
AN OBLIGATION
TO SERVE
THE WORLD."
- LEO BUSCAGLIA

Share Your Ideas

1.

2.

3.

4.

5.

Understanding Different Cultures

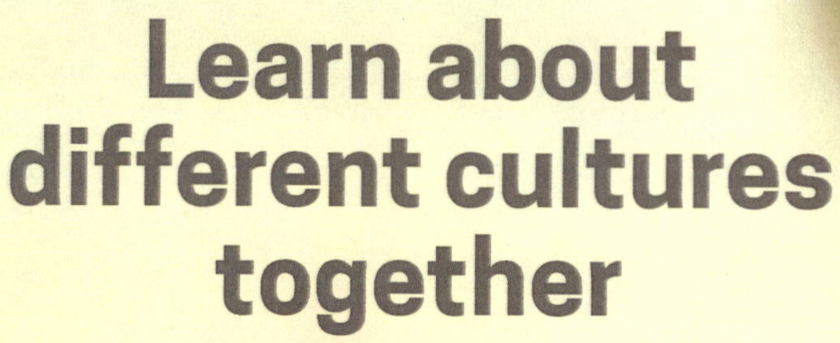

Learn about different cultures together

through food, music, art, and history.

ACTIVITY

Engagement Idea

- Host themed cultural nights.

- Cook traditional meals, listen to music, or create art from the chosen culture.

Words of Wisdom for Children

"THE BEAUTY OF THE WORLD LIES IN THE DIVERSITY OF ITS PEOPLE."

- UNKNOWN

Volunteer Projects

Engage in volunteer projects as a family.

Choose causes that resonate with all family members.

ACTIVITY

Engagement Idea

- Discuss the impact of your volunteer work.
- Encourage children to suggest volunteer activities.

Words of Wisdom for Children

"THE BEST WAY
TO FIND YOURSELF
IS
TO LOSE YOURSELF
IN
THE SERVICE OF OTHERS."
- MAHATMA GANDHI

Writing Workshops

Conduct family writing workshops.

Write stories, poems, or essays, then share them with each other.

ACTIVITY

Engagement Idea

- Create a family writing jar — each person adds a prompt and take turns picking one.
- Celebrate every piece of writing by displaying it somewhere in your home.

Words of Wisdom for Children

"WRITING IS AN EXPLORATION. YOU START FROM NOTHING AND LEARN AS YOU GO."

- E.L. DOCTOROW

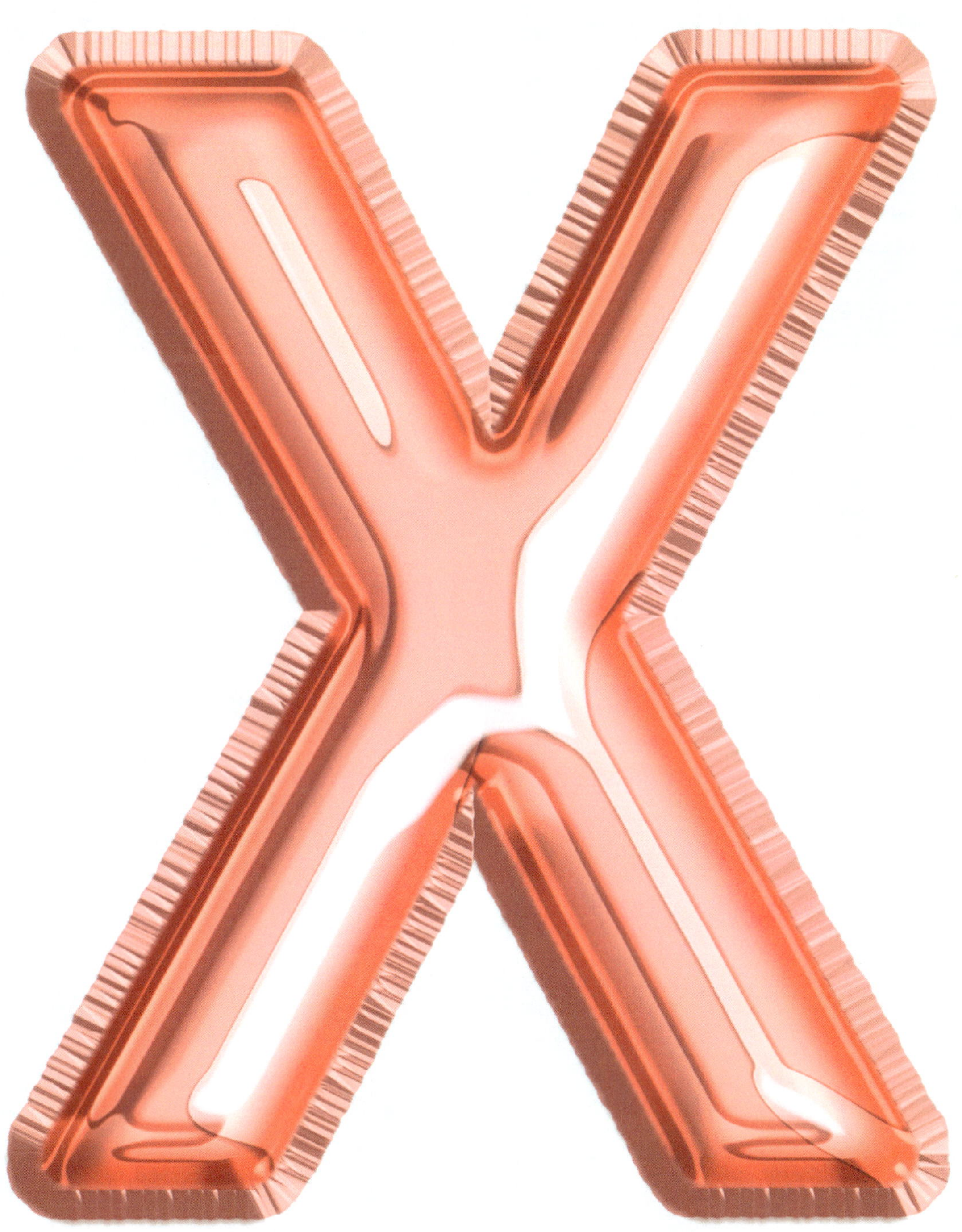

eXploring New Hobbies

Explore new hobbies together.

This could be anything from astronomy to baking to coding.

ACTIVITY

Engagement Idea

- Rotate choosing a new hobby to explore each month.
- Share what you love about each new hobby.

Words of Wisdom for Children

"HOBBIES ARE AN ESSENTIAL EXPRESSION OF ONE'S PASSION AND CURIOSITY."

- UNKNOWN

Share Your Ideas

1.

2.

3.

4.

5.

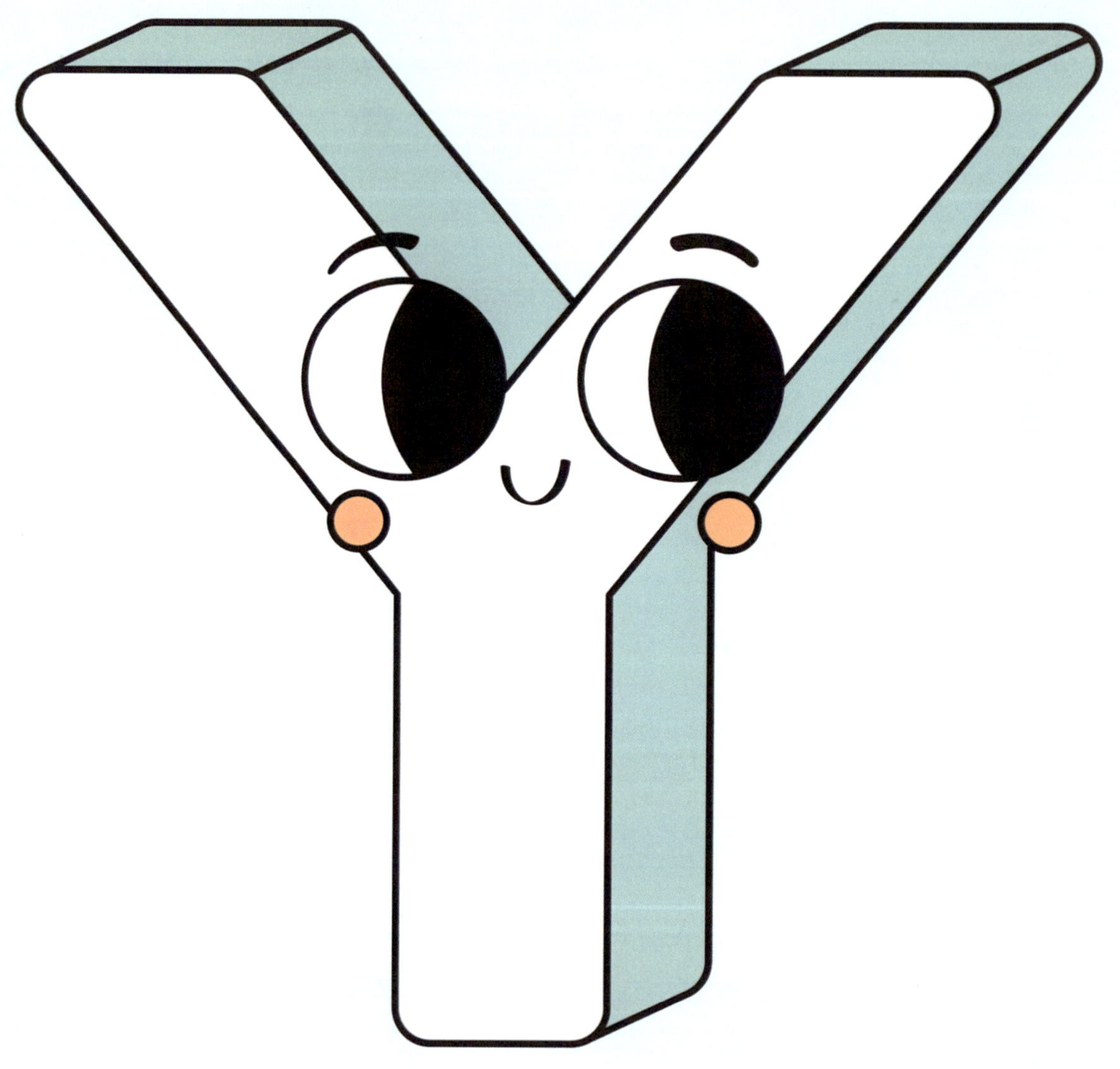

Yoga and Mindfulness Practice

Practice yoga and mindfulness together.

Focus on relaxation, breathing, and being present.

ACTIVITY

Engagement Idea

- Discuss the benefits of each session.
- Encourage each family member to lead a session.

Words of Wisdom for Children

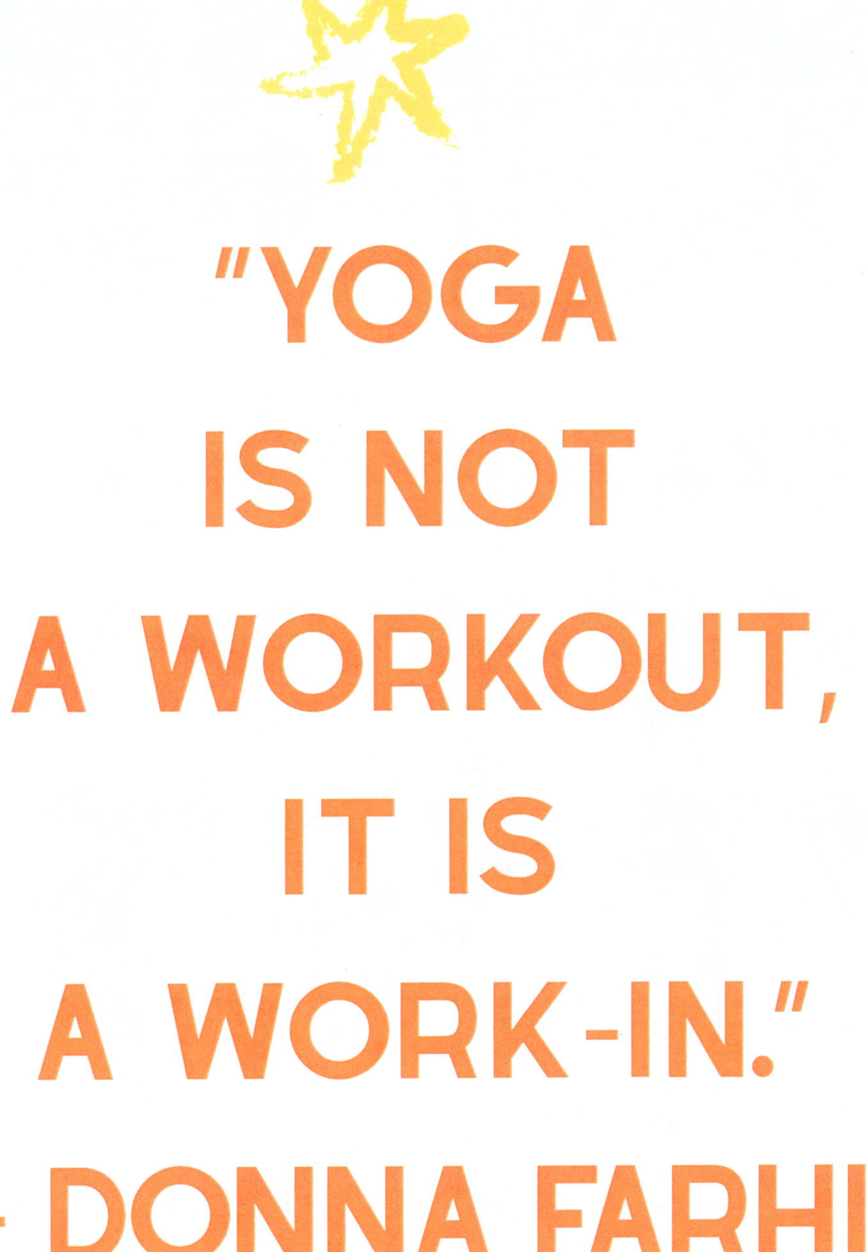

"YOGA
IS NOT
A WORKOUT,
IT IS
A WORK-IN."
- DONNA FARHI

Zero Waste Challenges

Undertake zero waste challenges.
Focus on reducing waste, recycling, and sustainable living.
ACTIVITY

Engagement Idea

- Set specific goals, like a plastic-free week.
- Discuss the environmental impact and personal learnings.

Words of Wisdom for Children

"ZERO WASTE ISN'T ABOUT WASTE DIVERSION. IT'S ABOUT REDESIGNING OUR ENTIRE CYCLE OF RESOURCE USE."

- BEA JOHNSON

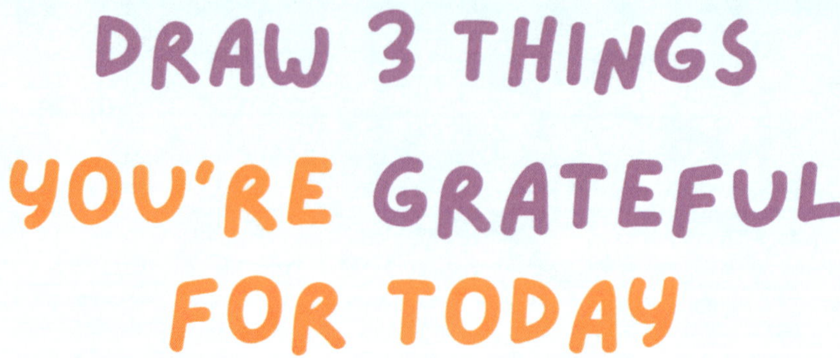
DRAW 3 THINGS
YOU'RE GRATEFUL
FOR TODAY

Share Your Ideas

1.

2.

3.

4.

5.

About the Author

LaBrita Andrews, Ed.M. is the creator of EVO 50™, a framework that helps parents understand the emotional weight children were never meant to carry and the relational conditions shaping a child's experience, and Team-Based Parenting™, the practice that helps parents build critical thinking, autonomy, and self-confidence in their children through everyday conversation.

Her work centers on one truth: children are often carrying emotional weight they were never meant to carry.

With more than 40 years of parenting experience — including 23 years as a stay-at-home mother and as the mother of five college-educated children — her understanding of family dynamics was built through lived experience first, and later strengthened through academic study.

She holds a Master's degree in Education Policy and Analysis from Harvard Graduate School of Education and is currently an Ed.D. doctoral student at Johns Hopkins School of Education.

Through her work, LaBrita helps parents recognize how communication, tone, and emotional responses influence how children develop confidence, autonomy, and the ability to think for themselves — while strengthening connection within the family.

The ABCs of Team-Based Parenting™: Family Journal for Kids brings this work into everyday life, giving families a hands-on way to practice connection, communication, and teamwork — one conversation at a time.

Thank you for journeying with us through The ABCs of Team-Based Parenting™: Family Journal for Kids.

May your family's adventures in learning and growing together continue to be as enriching and joyful as the moments shared within these pages.

Warm wishes,

LaBrita

www.ingramcontent.com/pod-product-compliance
Lightning Source LLC
Chambersburg PA
CBRC102034110726
48005CB00009BA/1027

* 9 7 9 8 9 9 5 4 8 7 9 1 3 *